MONSTER 4-WHEELERS

BY
Bill Holder

EDITED BY
Howard Schroeder, Ph.D.
Professor in Reading and Language Arts
Dept. of Curriculum and Instruction
Mankato State University

PUBLISHED BY
CRESTWOOD HOUSE
Mankato, MN, U.S.A.

CIP

LIBRARY OF CONGRESS CATALOGING IN PUBLICATION DATA

Holder, William G., 1937 -
  Monster 4-wheelers.

  (Super-charged!)
  Includes index.
  SUMMARY: Describes the design, capabilities, stunts, and popularity of the four-wheel drive trucks with giant wheels.
  1. Trucks—Four-wheel drive—Juvenile literature. [1. Trucks—Four wheel drive] I. Schroeder, Howard. II. Title. III. Title: Monster four-wheelers.
  TL230.5.F6H65   1987   629.2'23   87-15733
  ISBN 0-89686-353-0

International Standard Book Number:	Library of Congress Catalog Card Number:
0-89686-353-0	87-15733

CREDITS

Illustrations:
Cover Photo: Harry Dunn
John D. Farquhar: 4, 16, 20, 27, 33, 34, 36-37, 43, 44-45
Bill Holder: 7, 8, 11, 13, 15, 18-19, 22-23, 38
Harry Dunn: 24-25, 28
Suzy Hall: 30
F & A Photo: 40-41
Graphic Design & Production:
Baker Street Productions, Ltd.
Technical Assistance:
Steven Jacobsen

Copyright© 1987 by Crestwood House, Inc. All rights reserved. No part of this book may be reproduced in any form without written permission from the publisher, except for brief passages included in a review. Printed in the United States of America.

Box 3427, Mankato, MN, U.S.A. 56002

TABLE OF CONTENTS

Introduction 5
The Start................... 5
Bigfoot is Born 6
Other Tall Trucks 8
Building the Big Trucks 9
The Frame 10
The Motors 12
Powertrains 14
Tires and Suspension......... 15
Steering and Brakes 20
The Bodies 21
Crushing the Cars 26
Wheelstanding Monsters 29
Hooking to the Sled 31
Ramp Jumping 31
Hill Climbing 32
Mud and Water 32
Obstacle Courses 35
Monster Models............... 35
Tall-Truck Videos and TV 39
Strange Monsters 39
Glossary/Index 46-47

Monster four-wheelers are making their way all across the United States.

INTRODUCTION

Strange giants are rolling all across the United States. They are tall and wide, with enormous tires for moving them wherever they wish to go. Roaring loudly, they leave behind piles of twisted metal and shattered glass wherever they travel. From BIGFOOT to BARBARIAN, BEARFOOT to AWESOME KONG, the incredible giants are everywhere!

These are monster four-wheelers—the biggest and most famous vehicles ever to rumble on four wheels. They are truly huge. Some are as tall as fourteen feet (4.3 m), and almost as wide. Their amazing tires stand six feet (1.8 m) tall.

The strange world of monster machines is a trend unlike anything this country has ever seen. They attract people of all ages, from eight to eighty. Thousands of fans dream of owning or even driving one of these monsters. The giant trucks are one of a kind!

THE START

Monster truck excitement began about 1975, when four-wheel-drive trucks became popular. Four-wheel-drive means that all four wheels are helping pull the vehicle along. Soon the American people found out how much fun it was to go "four-wheeling." They could go to places they had never been.

For the first time, people realized that they could have a vehicle that was both fun and usable. What could be better than a four-wheel-drive truck? American automobile makers started turning out more of these trucks. People quickly started to buy them. Small or large, it didn't make any difference. Americans wanted these trucks.

Soon, four-wheel-drive truck clubs began to form all over the country. Club outings became popular get-togethers. People kept an eye on this quickly growing division of the vehicle industry. They wondered what would happen next.

BIGFOOT IS BORN

One four-wheel-drive fan who really was caught up with the excitement was Bob Chandler of Hazelwood, Missouri. For fun, Chandler and his wife had bought a truck in the late 1960's. Then he and a few of his friends formed a small four-wheel-drive shop. They started making parts and accessories for their favorite vehicles.

Chandler didn't have much money to advertise the products he was making for use in four-wheel-drive trucks. So to demonstrate his new products, he started taking his trucks to shows.

Finding the best way of testing the new parts led

BIGFOOT was the monster truck that started it all.

Chandler to conduct some experiments with old military equipment. Using those very strong parts let Chandler do some amazing things with his truck. He tested the truck very hard and ended up destroying many of the parts. Chandler's shop foreman told him that he had a "big foot" that was always planted flat down on the accelerator pedal. The name stuck, and BIGFOOT was born.

Chandler then installed four huge tires. He and his truck were instantly famous. His out-of-proportion truck became the talk of the four-wheel-drive world. "Have you seen BIGFOOT?" became one of the most-asked questions at all the national off-road events and mud-racing meets.

OTHER TALL TRUCKS

Good ideas quickly get copied, and it wasn't long before other people started building their own monster

Bob Chandler's BIGFOOT was instantly famous.

machines. Although Chandler was months ahead of the other builders, he actually helped his rivals in the development of their trucks. Men like Fred Shafer (BEARFOOT), Jeff Dane (KING KONG), and Everett Jasmer (USA-1) were the builders of the next family of monsters.

This was the first phase in monster truck development. It took place in the mid-to-late 1970's. These men and their first trucks were the forerunners of today's ever-growing numbers of monster trucks and their owners.

Presently, there are two hundred or more of the trucks around, and the number keeps growing. As long as they are popular, they will continue to be built. Some will succeed, while others will fall by the wayside.

It all began with the experiments of Bob Chandler, the father of the monsters.

BUILDING THE BIG TRUCKS

Despite their unusual appearance, these tall trucks actually have the same types of parts that all four-wheel-drive trucks have. Parts that turn the wheels of an ordinary Chevy or Ford truck are also needed on the monster machines. These parts, however, have to be a lot stronger for the monsters.

Of course, there are other differences between regular

trucks and the monsters. Turning those giant wheels takes a lot of power. These trucks do a lot more than just roll along. They go through huge mud pits, pull themselves up to wheelstands, and roll over piles of old cars. During many of these tricks, the huge engines are working at top power. The tricks often push the engines to their limits.

Monster trucks can weigh up to fifteen thousand pounds (6,804 kg). That's as much as six times heavier than your family car! It's easy to see why so much power is needed, and why the parts sending that power to the wheels have to be so strong.

THE FRAME

There is a lot involved in building one of these trucks, and it all begins with the frame. The frame supports the truck's total weight. Many tall-truck builders design their own frames from scratch. They may begin by welding two frames together. Others strengthen the original frame of their truck. No matter how they build the frames, the builders make them very strong. When a seven- or eight-ton (6 or 7 MT) vehicle comes down from a high jump, it must be built so that it won't bend or break.

Some of the monster-machine builders start with frame parts that come out of old army trucks. Then they change them for their own needs. Anything that will

*Monster frames have to be built **tough!***

make the truck stronger is tried by the builders. And yet some trucks still get their frames bent during shows. Monster trucks have also been known to break into two pieces. For example, the OUTLAW 35 truck from Florida was standing straight up on its rear wheels in a show. When it came down, it was broken in two!

THE MOTORS

Mounted to those strong frames is the most important part of the truck: the powerful motor. It seems that every builder has a different idea of the best way to get that power. Most of the monsters use either a Chevy or Ford engine that is "souped up" in many different ways. These motors are also much bigger than car motors that can be bought today.

Special pistons, connecting rods, and camshafts are added for strength and power. These are the same types of changes that are made for drag-racing and truck-pulling motors. Chevy motors are the most popular, but a number of the trucks—including BIGFOOT—use Ford engines.

Many of the motors use devices known as superchargers, or blowers. When the blowers come on, they push more air into the motor. This can increase the power of the engines by hundreds of horsepower. Supercharged engines can have over a thousand horsepower, compared to non-blown engines which have about six hundred horsepower.

Another way the engine builders increase the power of the engines is to "bore them out." This means that the cylinders containing the pistons are drilled out to bigger diameters, and bigger pistons are put inside. This change gives more power to the engines.

Not every tall truck has the great power boost provided

A giant motor is the most important part of a monster four-wheeler. This engine may have over a thousand horsepower.

by the supercharger. Some of these big machines increase their power with a nitrous oxide system. This system adds nitrous oxide, a gas, to the fuel, making it burn hotter and more powerfully. The system can add as much as two hundred horsepower to some engines.

Some motors also use fuel injection systems. Others use carburetors. Some of the monsters' motors burn gasoline, while others burn alcohol. The drivers like alcohol because it produces more power without burning as hot as gasoline.

POWERTRAINS

The powertrain is the system that includes the engine and the many parts needed to get the power to the four wheels. First in the powertrain is the automatic transmission. Many of the trucks have had their transmissions changed to help them do their strange new jobs better. The purpose of the transmission, which is bolted to the back of the motor, is to select the proper gearing of the motor power.

Next is a box known as the transfer case. This unit splits the power into two shafts and sends it to both the front and rear sets of wheels. Some monsters have two transfer cases for extra strength. Because the trucks are sitting so high, it may be necessary to use "drop boxes" which lower the drive shafts.

Then it's on to the front and rear differentials (or rear ends). These units take the power from the transfer case, turn it around corners, and send it to all four wheels. At first, the monsters' rear ends came from regular road trucks. But now, some come from big military trucks. Other monsters use what are called planetary rear ends. Planetary rear ends are normally used in tractors. The axles connecting all of these parts are built of heavy-duty steel.

TIRES AND SUSPENSION

All of these power set-ups have one purpose: To drive those giant wheels on which the truck rests. The tires

A tall truck's shock absorbers help settle it down after a hard landing.

Huge tires—like this one—gave monster four-wheelers their name.

come in several sizes, but they are all very BIG! The most popular size seems to be the sixty-six-inch (168 cm) tire. That's five and one-half feet high, just a little shorter than an average-size adult! There are also seventy-three-inch (185 cm) tires.

The biggest tires, however, are carried by one of the BIGFOOT trucks. (There are many versions of monster trucks that carry the famous "Bigfoot" name.) These amazing tires, ten feet (3 m) in diameter, weigh about two thousand pounds (907 kg). They once belonged to giant ice vehicles in Alaska during World War II.

Because of their weight and size, monster tires are very hard to handle when they are off the truck. During travel, the tires have to be removed, since they would make the trucks too tall to pass under bridges on their trailers. The trucks look strange sitting on normal-sized tires when they are hauled across the country from show to show.

Keeping these high-perched bodies stable is the job of the trucks' very complex suspension systems. Sitting so much higher than normal trucks, the tall trucks use as many as nine shock absorbers per wheel. These help settle it down when the truck lands from a high jump. Settling down fifteen thousand pounds (6,804 kg) is not an easy job. The springs, specially built, are very stiff and strong.

This BIGFOOT truck has the biggest tires of all.

Many tall trucks can hydraulically lift their bodies, hoods, and beds. Here HERCULES II shows off its monster parts.

STEERING AND BRAKES

In order for these trucks to perform tricks, they must have a good steering system. Most of them have independent steering for the front and back wheels. Some of them can turn within their own length. The trucks can also keep the body pointed straight while

20

moving at an angle. This is called "crab walking." It's a very strange sight indeed!

Getting one of these monsters stopped is a very tough job. Most of these monster trucks use huge disc brakes on all four wheels. Some trucks have a device called a driveline brake. This device presses on the drive shaft to stop the truck.

THE BODIES

The bodies of the tall trucks are of many shapes and styles. Some are not even from trucks at all. Monster machines have carried old and new car bodies and van bodies. The bodies are always brightly painted so that their many fans can tell them apart.

With the driver sitting high in the air, safety is a big concern. The floors in the bodies are strengthened to help protect the driver in case the powertrain below would fail. If this were to happen, parts could explode in all directions. There may also be a heavy roll cage or roll bars built around the driver. They would protect the driver should the truck flip over.

A metal drive-shaft loop contains the drive shaft and a protective shield around the transmission. Most monster trucks also carry fire extinguishers, and many of the drivers wear racing helmets.

From custom paint to polished chrome, tall-truck owners take good care of their monsters.

Many of the trucks can hydraulically lift their bodies off the frame. Others can lift the hood and bed separately.

Special lighting is another feature on many of these machines. Most tall trucks carry a row of high-intensity lights across the top of the cab. These lights raise the total height of many trucks to as much as fourteen feet (4.3 m). Other trucks have flashing marker lights all

over the body.

    The drivers of these trucks pay attention to beauty as well as strength. Chrome and polished metal are everywhere. The wheels, roll bars, and even the engine glisten brightly in the sunlight. When a truck costs as much as one hundred thousand dollars, every detail is important.

This monster truck seems to be waiting for its chance to play.

CRUSHING THE CARS

For a long time, a monster truck's claim to fame was its size and power. But just rolling around on the sixty-six-inch (168 cm) tires didn't keep the fans interested. It wasn't enough to look good. These monsters needed to get out and play!

Before long, many of the monsters were crushing cars. The sounds of flying glass and crushing metal filled the air from coast to coast. It looks easy, but crushing a row of cars isn't as simple as it looks.

Many of the monster drivers prefer certain brands of cars to crush. The cars, however, all need to be the same style, such as all sedans or station wagons. They also need to be about the same length so that the big trucks won't slip off the pile.

The crew at a truck show also does several things to the cars before they are crushed. First, all four tires are punctured so that the cars won't move around when the monster is on top of them. The car's radio antenna and the air cleaner stud are also removed. These could puncture one of the very expensive truck tires.

The TAURUS monster has carried the car-crushing act one step further. Instead of cars, its driver uses old school buses! This is a very dangerous trick. The TAURUS is high in the air when it is on top of the buses. It's a very long drop to the ground, and great care must be taken. The driver of TAURUS is currently the only one doing this trick.

Crunch!

The GOLIATH monster does another strange trick. The Ohio-based tall truck actually tears old cars into two pieces! A chain is hooked to the car and then attached to a solid object, such as a heavy tractor-pulling sled. Another chain is then hooked to the other end of the car and then to GOLIATH. With a slack in the chain, the eight-ton (7 MT) GOLIATH takes off. The car is torn apart by the power of the truck.

TAURUS does its favorite trick—crushing school buses.

To anyone who has ever been caught in rush-hour traffic, or been stuck behind a slow driver, the popularity of car crushing is understandable. People wish they could drive over the *top* of other cars and be on their way. The monster trucks fulfill that desire. The sound of crushing metal and glass seems to excite everybody.

WHEELSTANDING MONSTERS

What else can tall trucks do? The driver of LI'L BEARFOOT found out quite by accident that these trucks could stand up on their rear wheels. Wheelstanding (or wheelies) was born.

The giant trucks are well suited to do this kind of trick. With their short wheelbases, powerful motors and big tires, the tall trucks are perfect for the stunt.

As with all the monster tricks, it wasn't long before all the big trucks were doing wheelies. Some trucks have also done reverse wheelies, with the rear wheels instead of the front ones high up in the air. Other drivers have even approached stacks of cars in that reverse manner. The drivers of these great monsters are always looking for something new to do—and they usually seem to find it!

Another trick is a wheelie offshoot, first performed by the SAMSON I monster. This truck not only does a wheelstand, but throws itself over a stack of cars after making a run at them.

Pulling-trucks and tractors have long been known for carrying their front ends completely off the ground for the length of the three-hundred-foot (91 m) pulling track. Several monsters can do this, too—without pulling anything! One truck, the ACES HIGH, can go that distance with its front tires six feet (1.8 m) in the air.

Pulling a heavy sled is one of the toughest jobs of a monster four-wheeler.

The drivers of monster trucks have kept getting more and more daring. Many people knew that sooner or later, one of the tall trucks was going to stand too tall and fall. This has happened a number of times, with the trucks landing upside down. Seven to eight tons (6-7 MT) is a lot of weight to come crashing down. That's what the roll bars or cages are for—to protect the drivers.

HOOKING TO THE SLED

Because monster trucks often appear in truck and tractor pulls, it is not surprising that the high-risers are asked to hook up to the pulling sleds. Monster drivers will tell you that pulling the sled is one of the hardest things the big trucks can do.

Getting those giant wheels turning is hard enough. But adding thousands of pounds to pull along behind is really rough! Still, the trucks make it look easy.

BIGFOOT was the first truck to do the sled trick. In fact, the truck did the trick with its front end in the air.

RAMP JUMPING

One of the hardest tricks these drivers have begun doing is jumping from a ramp and flying high through the air. The HERCULES truck flies as high as eight feet (2.4 m) on some jumps. A number of monsters have bent their frames doing this trick. The trucks must have many shock absorbers to soften the landings!

The parts of the truck that take most of the force of these jumps are the tires and wheels. These tires, which were built for farm tractors and not jumping monsters, have been known to burst. The wheels supporting them have been bent and even crushed.

HILL CLIMBING

During the summer of 1986, the famous 180-foot (55 m) hill at Cleves, Ohio, was the site of a very interesting competition. The hill had been used for years by four-wheel-drive trucks trying to make it to the top. It wasn't easy, since the entire hill was covered with pea gravel (small, round stones.)

Welcome BIGFOOT! Along with ten monsters that were on hand that day, BIGFOOT again proved its power by blasting to the top after a couple of tries. It was the only one able to make it to the top. In 1987, the trucks came back, and this time USA-1, along with BIGFOOT, was able to make it to the top.

The drivers of the tall trucks also drag-raced with each other for the first time. It was done uphill on one of the smaller hills at the off-road course. The big trucks showed that they could do this task, too. What would be next?

MUD AND WATER

How about putting them in the mud? That would certainly be different. Some of the monsters have done "mud bogging," but not very many. The idea of having to clean the trucks up really makes the monster owners think a long time about doing it. But it is quite a sight when one of them gets going in the mud. Huge hunks of dirt are thrown up by the giant spinning tires. It's great fun for everyone—except for the people who have to clean up the trucks afterwards!

Then there's the water. Amazingly, some of these huge, heavy trucks can float. There have been some monster races in rivers and lakes. The giant tires act like strange paddle wheels and slowly push the trucks along.

BEARFOOT has shown a number of times that it can float and do it well. It's one of the best. Sometimes, though, the tricks don't turn out as expected. The

Will this tall truck make it to the top of the hill?

Crushing cars is just one of the many tricks in an obstacle course.

CARDIFF GIANT monster tried a floating act in 1982, and completely turned over. As if in slow motion, the truck started rolling over. Finally, all that could be seen were the bottoms of the four tires. They stuck up from the water like the backs of four huge turtles.

OBSTACLE COURSES

Promoters recently decided that it would be fun to combine the monster tricks into one event. Obstacle courses were laid out in the big stadiums where the trucks usually performed. The courses had piles of cars to crush, hills to climb, mud to drive through, and even sleds to pull. The first truck to cross the finish line was declared the winner. In some of these monster challenges, as many as ten or twelve of the big trucks competed. It's a show that has been very popular with the fans.

Large crowds attend these shows. Sometimes as many as ninety thousand people fill the stadiums. The drivers try hard to win with their machines, because the winners are invited back to other shows. Many of the drivers make their living from their trucks, so having many show dates is very important.

The tricks of the monster trucks continue to get more difficult. But not all trucks can do all of the tricks. Some may fall by the wayside. There are hundreds of trucks out there, and they are all quite a sight to see. But just looking good is no longer enough. They have to be able to perform.

MONSTER MODELS

With the great popularity of monster machines, toy builders soon saw a chance to bring the trucks to chil-

A monster four-wheeler can go fast when it wants to!

Giant trucks are the bigger-than-life stars in these videotapes.

dren. It wasn't long before there were models of BIGFOOT, STOMPER BULLY, BEARFOOT, EAGLE, USA-1 and others on toy shelves all over the country. There were also a number of monster truck models that didn't look like any particular real monster.

Some of these models are motorized—and a few are even radio-controlled. It's a strange sight to see these little mini-monsters doing the same tricks as the big ones.

TALL-TRUCK VIDEOS AND TV

After the toys came videos of the big trucks. One of the most famous was a video by the ZZ Top rock group that featured BEARFOOT for two and a half minutes. Later, BIGFOOT starred with another rock group in a music video.

Tall trucks have starred in their own video specials as well. "The Battle of the Monster Trucks," "Revenge of the Monster Trucks," and "The Final Chapter" have all been best-sellers, attracting buyers of all ages.

Some monster four-wheelers, such as USA-1 and BIGFOOT, have even appeared in TV commercials.

STRANGE MONSTERS

Just like any other type of automotive vehicle, there are a few monsters that are completely different from the "standard" monsters.

Three of these don't have any wheels at all—yet they still do car crushing. How? The VIRGINIA BEACH BEAST, HEAVY CHEVY, and CAR KILLER use tank treads to move.

The motors in these vehicles are standard car motors. They sit backwards in the rear of the vehicle. The front sprockets of the tanks are powered, making these trucks the only front-wheel-drive monsters.

HEAVY CHEVY is a different breed of tall truck—it uses tank treads instead of tires.

The treads for these strange monsters came from World War II tanks and are over forty years old. The weight of the tread and the carriage assembly makes these trucks much heavier than other monster trucks. They often weigh twelve or thirteen tons (11-12 MT). Needless to say, they can quickly flatten cars to only about a foot (30 cm) high.

Some monsters are actually semi trucks. The most famous is the KING OF THE ROAD vehicle. It can do many of the things the normal monsters do.

Monster vans? Yes, there are a number of van bodies sitting atop big wheels. Some of the best known are the LEAD BUTTERFLY, THE QUADRAVAN and the BARBARIAN. A van body sitting on top of a set of monster wheels gives the vehicle a completely different look!

Using a car body instead of a truck body is another trend that's been happening with the monsters. The two most famous of these machines are the MONSTER VETTE and BLUE THUNDER. These vehicles use the bodies of a new Corvette and a 1968 Camaro. There's also the CAJUN KING, which has a 1976 Cadillac body.

Several types of motors are being used by the monsters as well. Not surprisingly, several truck owners have gone to using two engines. Both the GOLIATH and the MEGAFORCE trucks have two engines. One is in the normal location under the hood and the other is mounted in the bed of the truck. In both cases, the total power is close to two thousand horsepower.

The ROLLIN' THUNDER monster does not use a gasoline engine, like most of these vehicles. Instead, it uses a giant diesel engine. Then, there's AWESOME KONG II, which uses a World War II aircraft engine. Who knows what's next?

The strange, and the *very* strange, monsters have appeared.

They are truly the rage of the 1980's. Their noise, power and amazing tricks make them exciting to all of us!

This monster has the body of a van.

43

For thousands of fans, the strange world of monster four-wheelers can't be beat!

GLOSSARY / INDEX

CAR CRUSHING 26, 28, 35, 39 — *The first of the many monster-truck tricks, and still the most popular.*

CARBURETOR 14 — *The part of the engine that feeds the fuel/air mixture to the cylinders.*

FOUR-WHEEL DRIVE 5, 6, 8, 9 — *A type of vehicle in which all four wheels are driving.*

HORSEPOWER 12, 14, 43 — *The way the power of an engine is measured.*

"MUD BOGGING" 32, 35 — *The act of driving the monster trucks through large areas of mud.*

NITROUS OXIDE SYSTEM 14 — *A system that adds nitrous oxide to the engine, increasing the engine's power.*

OBSTACLE COURSE 35 — *A series of obstacles faced by the monsters as they compete against each other. Tasks include piles of cars to crush, steep hills to climb, tight corners to turn, and mud pits to cross.*

POWERTRAIN 14, 21 — *Includes the engine, transmission, transfer case, drive shafts, axles, and rear ends.*

PULLING 12, 29, 31, 35 — *In this monster-truck trick, the truck is hooked to a pulling sled to see how far it can be pulled.*

GLOSSARY / INDEX

REAR END (Differential) 14, 15 — *This unit turns the power from the transfer case out to the rear wheels.*

SHOCKS 17, 31 — *Units that settle down the truck after coming down from a jump.*

"SOUPING UP" 12 — *Changing an engine to make it more powerful.*

SPRINGS 17 — *Pieces of steel laid together that cushion the truck when it performs tricks.*

SUPERCHARGER 12, 14 — *A device mounted to the top of the motor that pumps in more air and provides more power.*

TRANSFER CASE 14 — *This device takes the power from the transmission and then separates it to two drive shafts for each set of giant wheels.*

TRANSMISSION 14, 21 — *Mounted to the back of the motor, this unit gears the power from the engine.*

WHEELSTAND (Wheelie) 10, 29 — *The truck stands up on its rear (or front) tires.*